Solo
repertoire
FOR THE YOUNG PIANIST

Compiled and Edited by

William Gillock

ISBN 978-1-4950-3473-2

EXCLUSIVELY DISTRIBUTED BY

WILLIS MUSIC

HAL•LEONARD®

Visit Hal Leonard Online at
www.halleonard.com

Contact us:
Hal Leonard
7777 West Bluemound Road
Milwaukee, WI 53213
Email: info@halleonard.com

In Europe, contact:
Hal Leonard Europe Limited
42 Wigmore Street
Marylebone, London, W1U 2RN
Email: info@halleonardeurope.com

In Australia, contact:
Hal Leonard Australia Pty. Ltd.
4 Lentara Court
Cheltenham, Victoria, 3192 Australia
Email: info@halleonard.com.au

Contents

King Winter

John Thompson

Rollicky

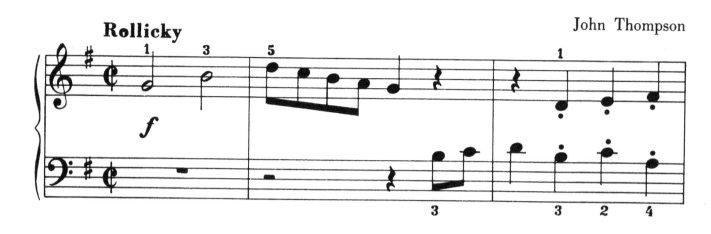

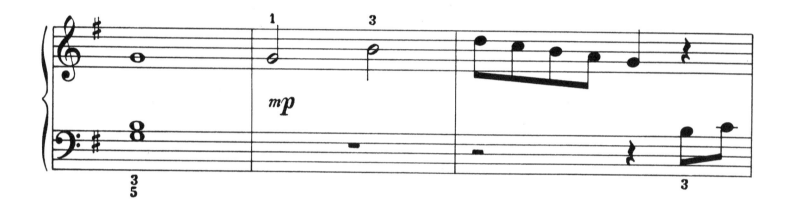

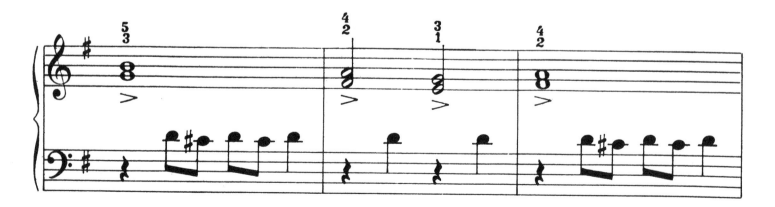

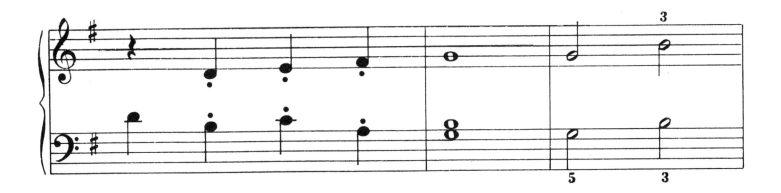

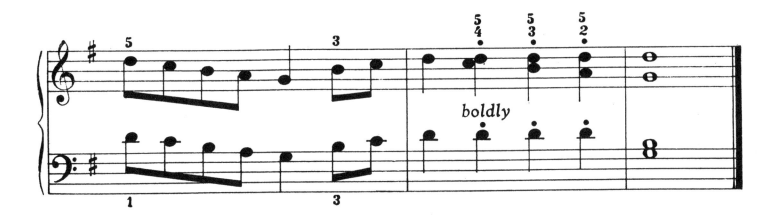

Lullaby

John Cacavas

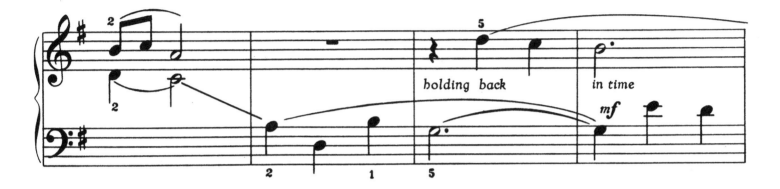

Dance To The Bagpipe

Alexander Goedicke

Lively, with a heavy beat

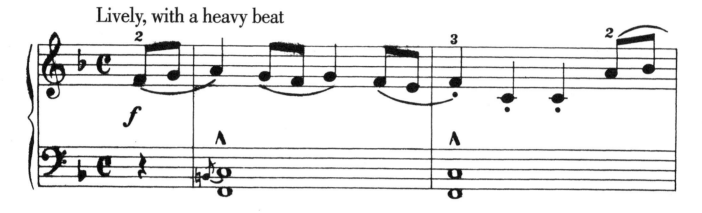

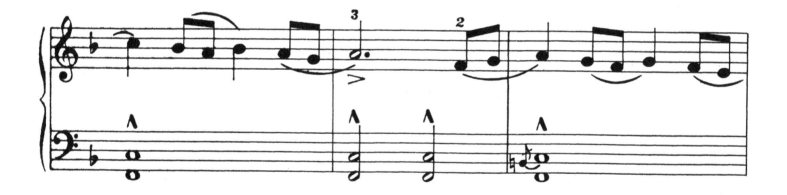

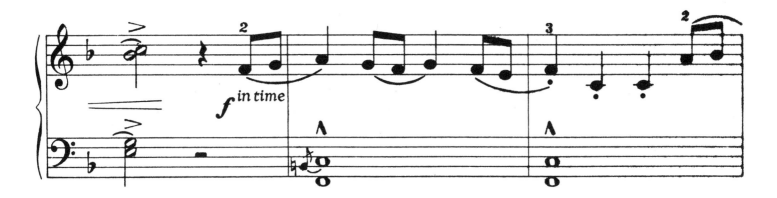

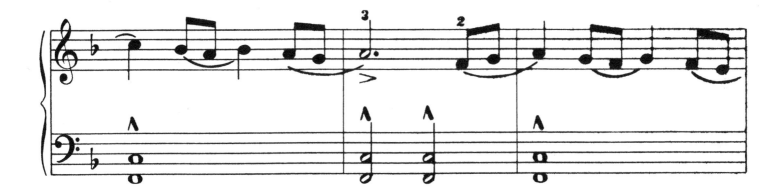

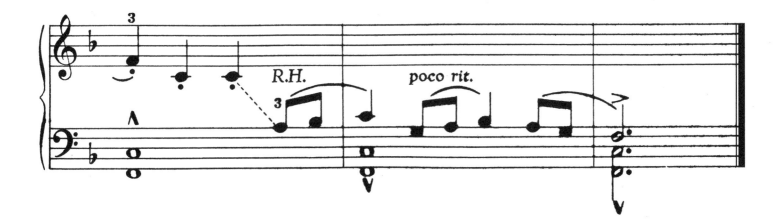

Playground Frolic

T. Salutrinskaya

With spirit

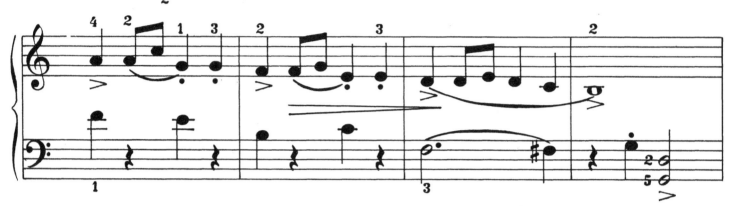

Gavotte

George Phillip Telemann

In a jovial mood

By Sylvan Lake

Esther Benson

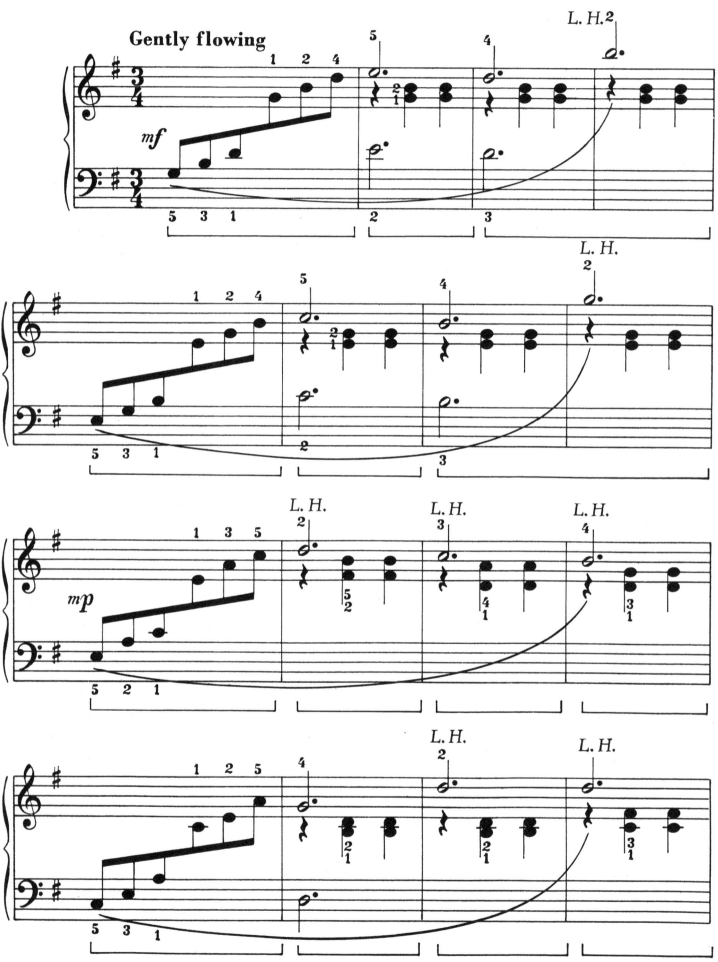

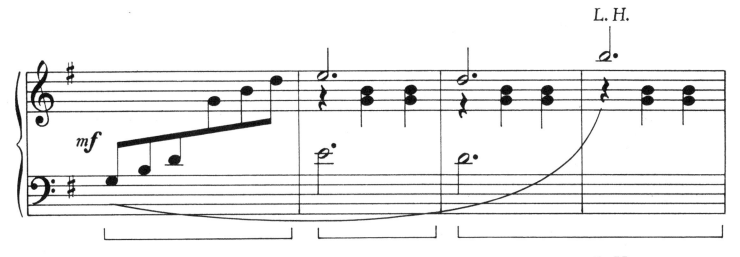

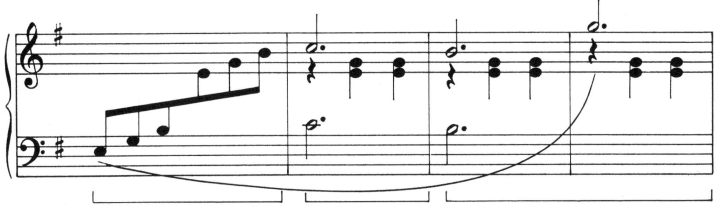

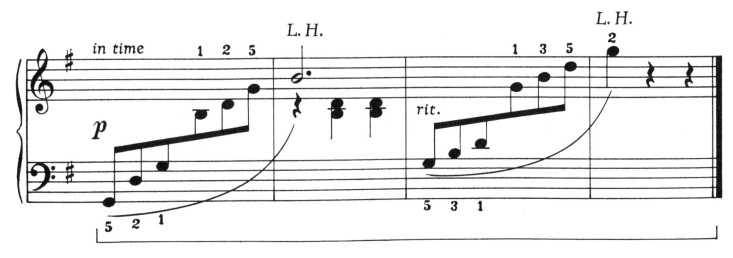

Scotch Dance

W. E. Robinson

Bagpipes

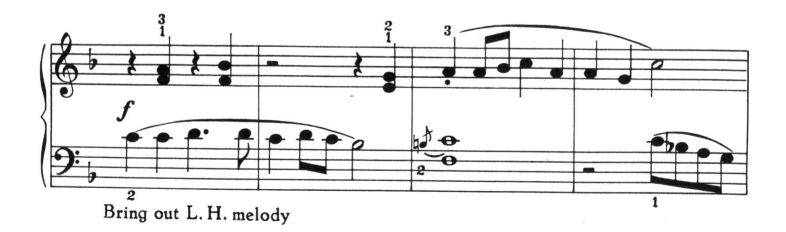

Bring out L. H. melody

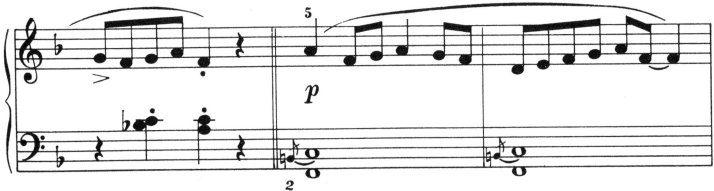

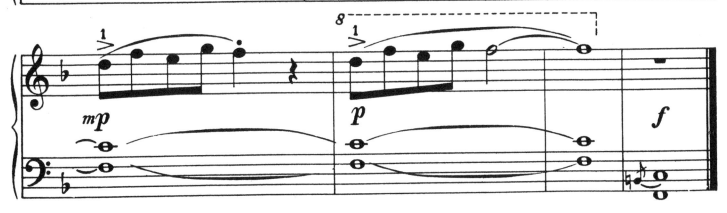

Mystic Night

Lydia Kircher

Left hand singing, and with expression

March Of The Tin Soldiers

Alexander Gretchaninoff

Vigorously, with steady motion

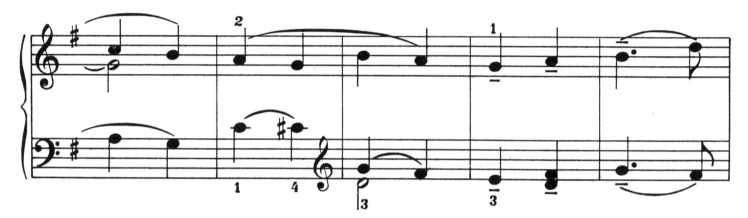

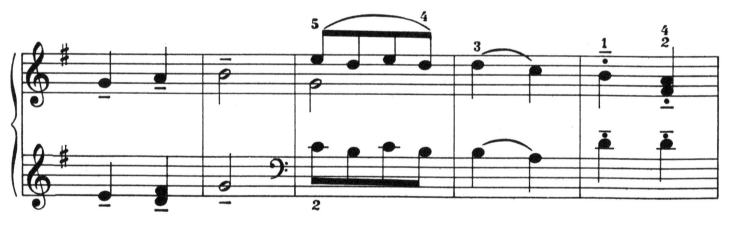

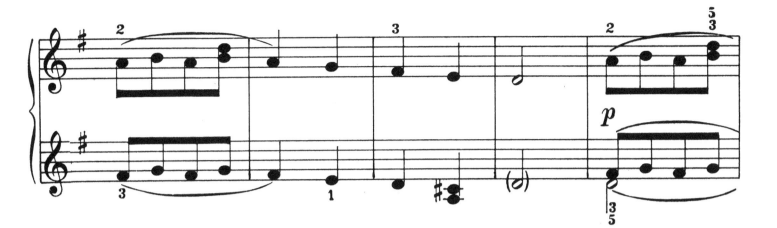

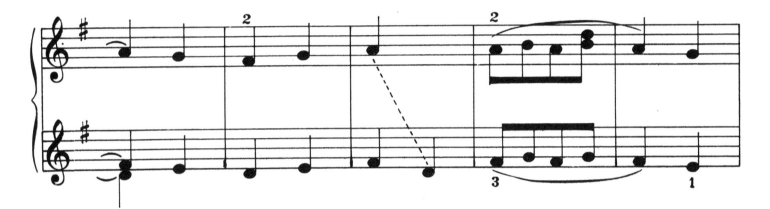

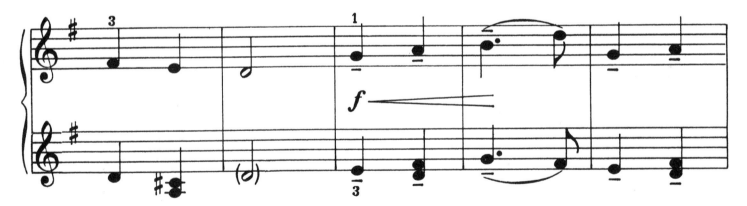

Bee, Bee, With Buzzing Wing

Moderately

Evalie Fisher

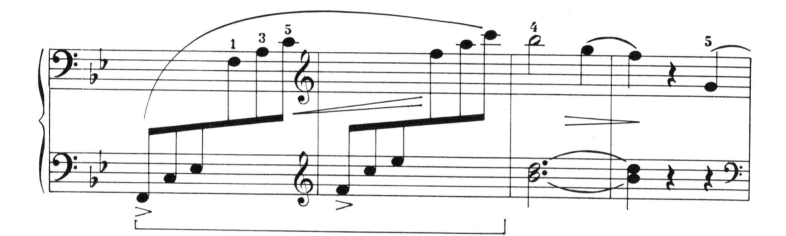

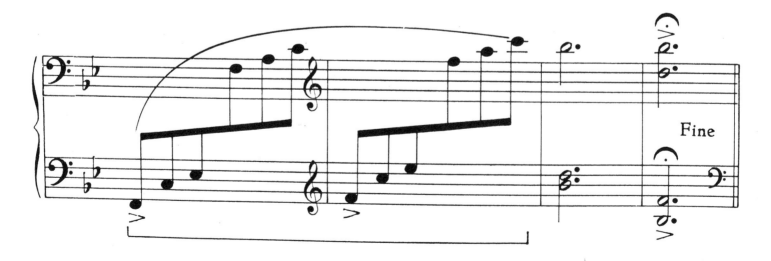

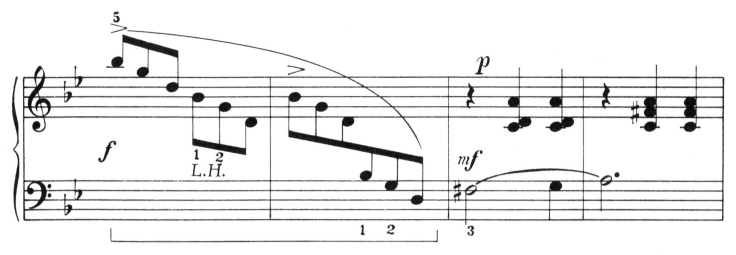

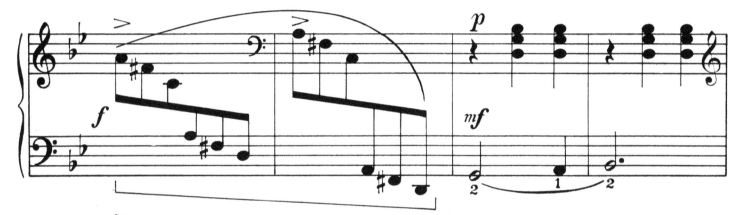

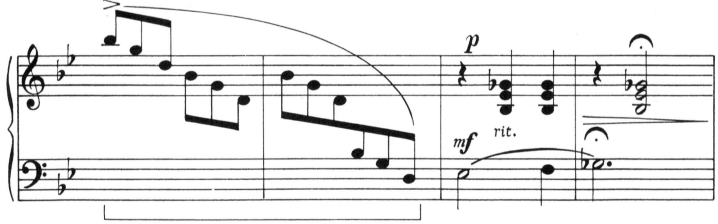

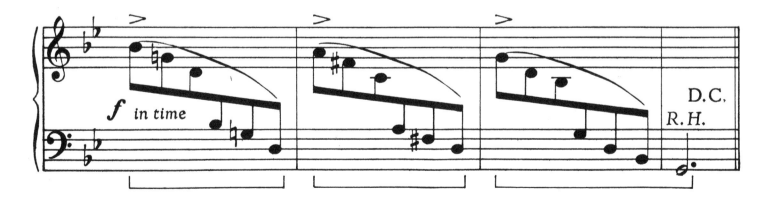

The Cuckoo's Call

Emil Söchting

Allegretto

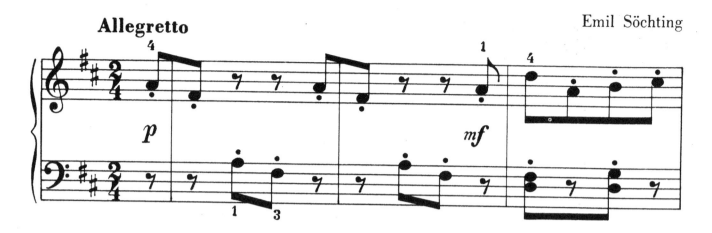

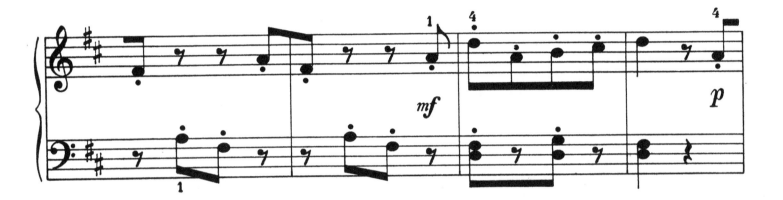

Jumbo

Lillian Miller

Heavily

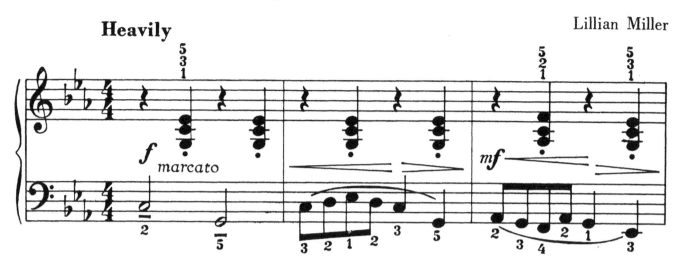

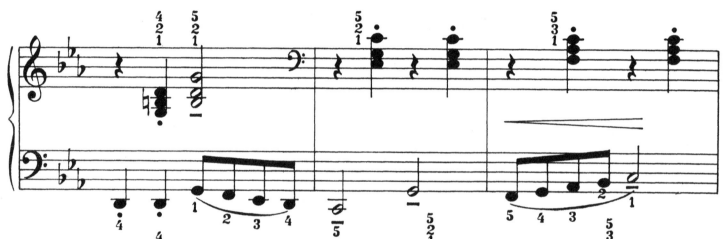

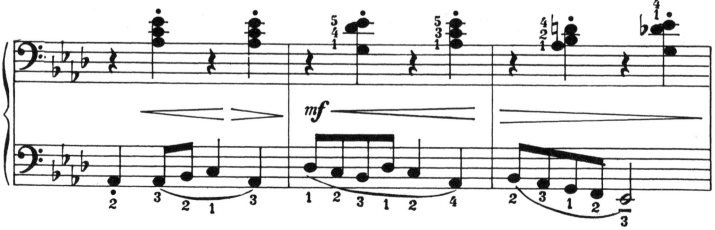

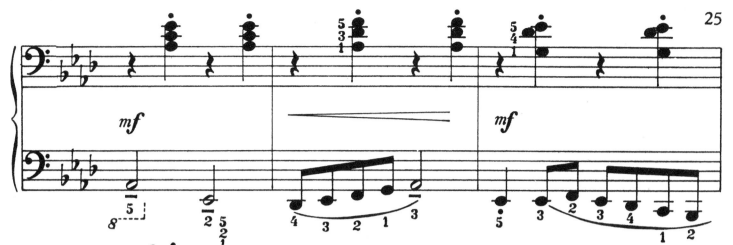

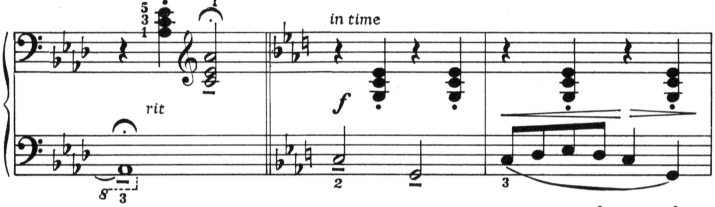

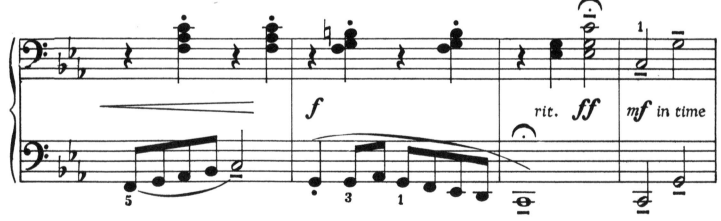

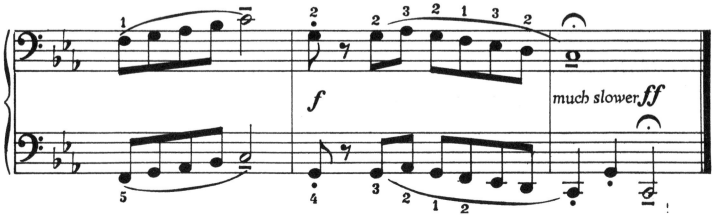

Little Waltz

With a gentle lilt

Dmitri Shostakovich

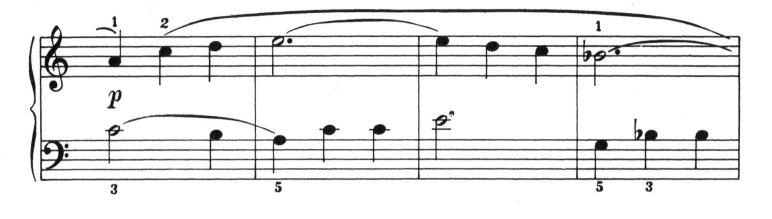

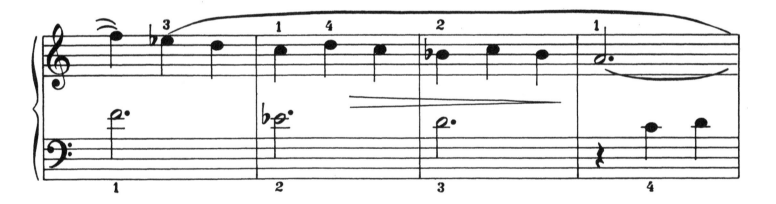

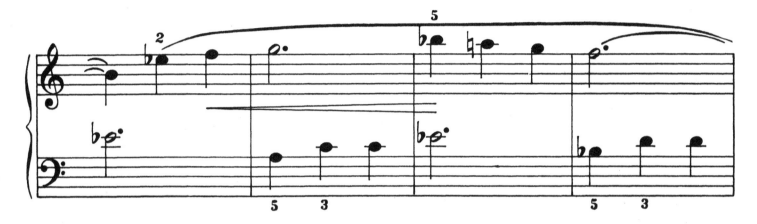

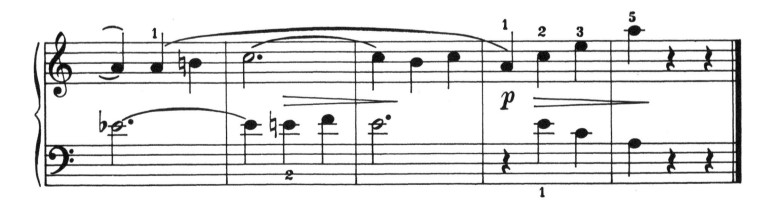

Swinging High And Low

Hazel Cobb

Moderately

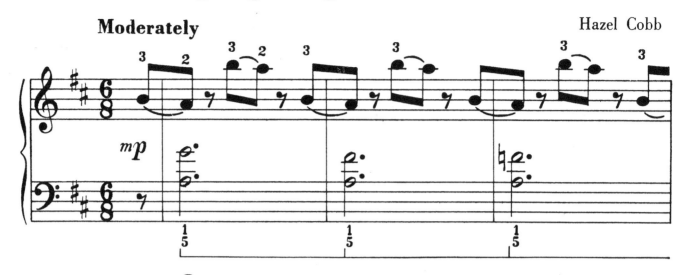

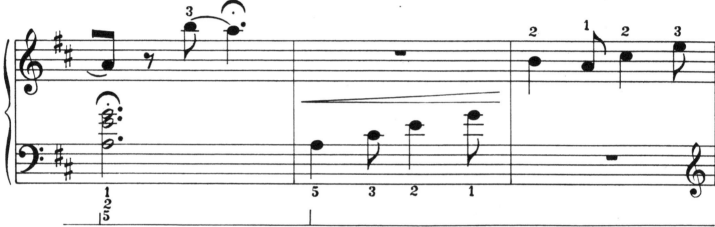

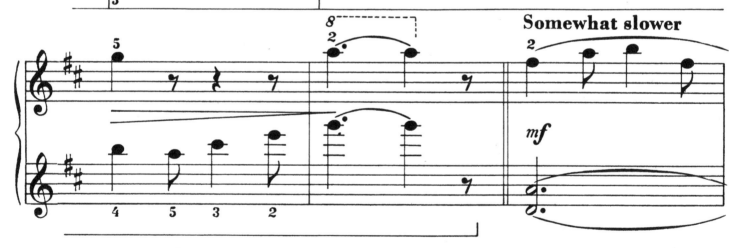

Somewhat slower

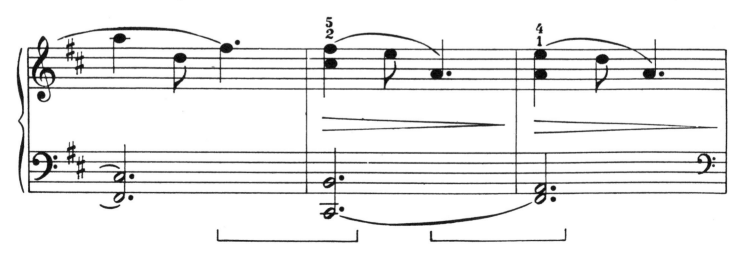

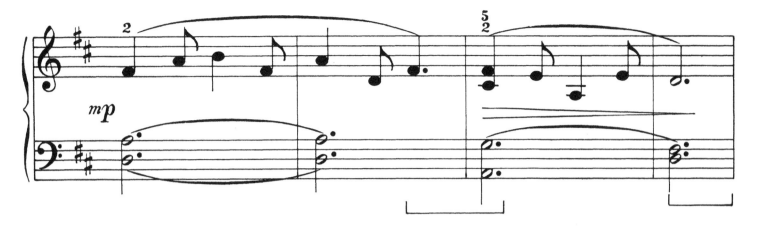

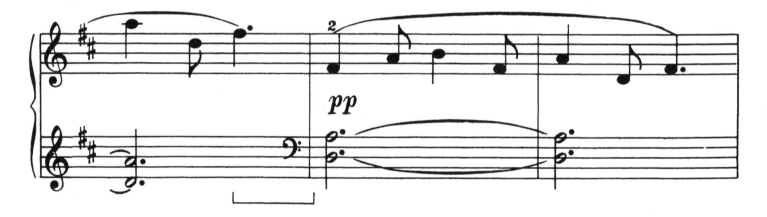

MUSIC FROM
William Gillock

Available exclusively from WILLIS MUSIC

"The Gillock name spells magic to teachers around the world..."
Lynn Freeman Olson, renowned piano pedagogue

NEW ORLEANS JAZZ STYLES
Gillock believed that every student's musical education should include experiences in a variety of popular stylings, including jazz, as a recurring phase of his or her studies. Students should also be encouraged to deviate from the written notes with their own improvisations if desired, for spontaneity is an essential ingredient of the jazz idiom.

Originals

NEW ORLEANS JAZZ STYLES
00415931 Book Only..$5.99

MORE NEW ORLEANS JAZZ STYLES
00415946 Book Only..$5.99

STILL MORE NEW ORLEANS JAZZ STYLES
00404401 Book Only..$5.99

NEW ORLEANS JAZZ STYLES - COMPLETE
00416922 Book/Audio $19.99

Duets *(arr. Glenda Austin)*

NEW ORLEANS JAZZ STYLES DUETS
00416805 Book/CD $9.99

MORE NEW ORLEANS JAZZ STYLES DUETS
00416806 Book/CD $9.99

STILL MORE NEW ORLEANS JAZZ STYLES DUETS
00416807 Book/CD $9.99

Simplified *(arr. Glenda Austin)*

SIMPLIFIED NEW ORLEANS JAZZ STYLES
00406603 ....$5.99

MORE SIMPLIFIED NEW ORLEANS JAZZ STYLES
00406604 ....$5.99

STILL MORE SIMPLIFIED NEW ORLEANS JAZZ STYLES
00406605 ....$5.99

ACCENT ON GILLOCK SERIES
Excellent piano solos in all levels by Gillock. Great recital pieces!
00405993	Volume 1 Book...........	$5.99
00405994	Volume 2 Book...........	$5.99
00405995	Volume 3 Book...........	$5.99
00405996	Volume 4 Book...........	$5.99
00405997	Volume 5 Book...........	$5.99
00405999	Volume 6 Book...........	$5.99
00406000	Volume 7 Book...........	$5.99
00406001	Volume 8 Book...........	$5.99

ACCENT ON CLASSICAL
Early to Mid-Intermediate Level
Gillock transformed several classical favorites into accessible teaching pieces, including Beethoven's "Für Elise" and "German Dance" (Op.17/9). Other pieces in this timeless collection include: Capriccietto • Barcarolle • Piece in Classic Style • Sonatina in C.
00416932 .... $8.99

ACCENT ON DUETS
Mid to Later Intermediate Level
Eight fantastic Gillock duets in one book! Includes: Sidewalk Cafe • Liebesfreud (Kreisler) • Jazz Prelude • Dance of the Sugar Plum Fairy (Tchaikovsky) • Fiesta Mariachi. A must-have for every piano studio.
00416804 1 Piano/4 Hands................................$12.99

00415712	Accent on Analytical Sonatinas...........EI	$5.99
00415797	Accent on Black Keys.....................MI	$5.99
00415748	Accent on Majors.........................LE	$5.99
00415569	Accent on Majors & Minors ....EI	$5.99
00415165	Accent on Rhythm & Style...............MI	$5.99

ACCENT ON SOLOS – COMPLETE
33 Pieces for the Advancing Young Pianist
A newly edited and engraved compilation of all 3 of Gillock's popular Accent on Solos books. These 33 short teaching pieces have been in print for over 50 years for a simple reason: the music continues to motivate piano students of every age!
00200896 Early to Later Elementary.....................$12.99

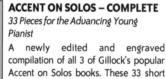

ACCENT ON TWO PIANOS
Four Original Pieces for 2 Pianos, 4 Hands
Titles: Carnival in Rio • On a Paris Boulevard • Portrait of Paris • Viennese Rondo. Includes a duplicate score insert for the second piano.

00146176 Intermediate to Advanced $9.99

ALSO AVAILABLE

FOUNTAIN IN THE RAIN
A sophisticated Gillock classic! Composed in 1960, this piece is reminiscent of impressionism and continues to be on annual recital lists. Students particularly enjoy the changing harmonies and nailing the splashy cadenza in the middle!
00414908..$3.99
00114960 Duet, arr. Glenda Austin $3.99

PORTRAIT OF PARIS
This beautiful composition evokes the romance of long-ago Paris, its eighth notes building gracefully to an incredibly satisfying climax of cascading notes. Excellent for bringing out top-voicing. Gillock has also written a second piano part that results in a very effective piano duo arrangement.
00414627..$2.99

THREE JAZZ PRELUDES
These preludes may be played as a set or as individual pieces. These dazzling pieces are Gillock at his best.
00416100..$3.99

CLASSIC PIANO REPERTOIRE – WILLIAM GILLOCK
Newly engraved and edited!

00416912 Intermediate to Advanced $12.99
00416957 Elementary $8.99

WILLIAM GILLOCK RECITAL COLLECTION
Features an extensive compilation of over 50 of William Gillock's most popular and frequently performed recital pieces. Newly engraved and edited to celebrate Gillock's centennial year.

00201747 Intermediate to Advanced $19.99

Find us online at
www.willispianomusic.com

0117